The Everyday Cooking Collection

ITALIAN
AROMAS

Licensed and produced by:

DIRECT SOURCE
SPECIAL PRODUCTS INC.

©℗1999 DIRECT SOURCE SPECIAL PRODUCTS INC.
Canada: P.O. Box 361,
Victoria Station, Westmount,
Quebec, Canada
H3Z 2V8
U.S.: P.O. Box 2189,
609 New York Road, Plattsburgh,
New York, 12903

Recipes and photos courtesy of:
Les Éditions Multi-Concept Inc.

Printed in Canada

ISBN# 1-896306-49-7

BAGNA ITALIAN STYLE

4 SERVINGS

Preparation Time: 20 minutes
Cooking Time: none

2 tbsp	(25 ml) olive oil
2 tbsp	(25 ml) lemon juice
2 tbsp	(25 ml) chopped, fresh parsley
1 tbsp	(15 ml) minced garlic
1 tsp	(5 ml) dried oregano
1 tsp	(5 ml) dried basil
4	slices of bread with sesame seeds, toasted
2 cans	(368 g) flaked tuna in water, drained
1/2 cup	(125 ml) cucumber, seeded and diced
2	tomatoes, seeded and diced
1/2 cup	(125 ml) diced green pepper
2	green onions, diced
1/4 cup	(50 ml) diced celery
	salt and pepper, to taste

GARNISH

2	hard boiled eggs, grated
8	anchovy filets (optional)
8	black olives, pitted
8	sprigs of parsley

In a small bowl, combine the oil, lemon juice, parsley, garlic, basil and oregano. Spread on the slices of bread and set aside.

In a bowl, mix together the tuna, cucumber, tomatoes, peppers, onions and celery; season.

Spread the tuna mixture on the bread. Cut each slice into 2 triangles and garnish with eggs, anchovies, black olives and parsley.

BARBECUED CANAPÉS

4 SERVINGS

Preparation Time: 10 minutes
Cooking Time: 10 minutes

4	slices of bread
1/3 cup	(75 ml) pesto
1/3 cup	(75 ml) olive oil
	salt and pepper, to taste
2	tomatoes, sliced
4 oz	(125 g) sliced prosciutto
4 oz	(125 g) sliced provolone cheese

Grill the bread slices on an oiled barbecue grill over medium heat.

Spread a mixture of pesto and olive oil on the bread; season. Garnish with tomato slices, prosciutto and provolone cheese.

Place on an aluminum plate and put back on to the barbecue. Close the lid and let the cheese melt over low heat. Cut each slice of bread into four triangles and serve.

FLORENTINE CREAM OF TOMATO SOUP

4 SERVINGS

Preparation Time: 15 minutes
Cooking Time: 25 minutes

1 tsp	(5 ml) vegetable oil
1/4 cup	(50 ml) chopped onions
1/2 cup	(125 ml) chopped celery
1	small garlic clove, minced
28 oz	(796 ml) can of crushed tomatoes
1 1/2 cups	(375 ml) chicken stock, skimmed of fat
1/4 cup	(50 ml) instant rice
1/2 tsp	(2 ml) dried oregano
1/2 tsp	(2 ml) dried basil
	salt and pepper, to taste
1 tbsp	(15 ml) cornstarch
1/4 cup	(50 ml) water
4	slices of french bread (baguette), slightly toasted
1/4 cup	(50 ml) mozzarella cheese
1/2	package of spinach, rinsed well, drained and slightly cooked
1/4 cup	(50 ml) sour cream

In a large pan, heat the oil and lightly sauté the onions and celery. Add the garlic, tomatoes, chicken stock, rice, oregano and basil. Season and let simmer for 20 minutes.

With a food processor or an electric mixer, purée the mixture and place it back in the pan. If necessary, thicken by adding cornstarch diluted in a little water. Keep warm.

Preheat the oven to broil. Garnish the bread slices with cheese, and place on a cookie sheet. Broil until golden.

When ready to serve, add the spinach and sour cream to the soup. Serve with the cheese baguette slices.

CAPICOLLO ROLL-UPS WITH PESTO

4 SERVINGS

Preparation Time: 20 minutes
Cooking Time: none

4 oz	(125 g) cream cheese
2 tbsp	(25 ml) softened butter
2 tbsp	(25 ml) pesto, homemade or store bought
4	slices of capicollo
8	green and black olives, chopped
1 tbsp	(15 ml) chopped, fresh parsley

VINAIGRETTE

1/4 cup	(50 ml) olive oil
1 tbsp	(15 ml) wine vinegar, red or white
1 tbsp	(15 ml) lemon juice
1 tbsp	(15 ml) pesto
	salt and pepper, to taste

GARNISH

3 cups	(750 ml) lettuce, of choice
4	cherry tomatoes
1 1/2 cups	(375 ml) marinated vegetables, Italian style (optional)
4	sprigs of fresh basil

In a food processor or with an electric mixer, mix together the cream cheese, butter and pesto.

Spread this mixture onto the capicollo slices; sprinkle with the crushed olives and parsley. Roll up each capicollo slice. Wrap the rolls in plastic wrap and refrigerate for 2 hours. You can place the rolls in the freezer which will accelerate the process.

VINAIGRETTE

In a bowl, mix together the olive oil, vinegar, lemon juice and pesto; season to taste.

GARNISH

Slice each capicollo roll . Line the plates with lettuce, divide the capicollo rolls equally among the plates and garnish with cherry tomatoes, marinated vegetables, pesto vinaigrette and a sprig of basil.

VEGETABLE SOUP

4 SERVINGS

Preparation Time: 15 minutes
Cooking Time: 30 minutes

1 tbsp	(15 ml) corn oil
1/2 cup	(125 ml) sliced leek
1	small onion, sliced
1/2 cup	(125 ml) chopped celery
1/2 cup	(125 ml) chopped carrots
6 cups	(1.5 L) chicken stock, skimmed of fat
1 cup	(250 ml) tortellini
	salt and pepper, to taste
1	medium egg
2 tbsp	(25 ml) chopped, fresh parsley
2 tbsp	(25 ml) chopped, fresh basil
1 tbsp	(15 ml) grated Parmesan cheese
4	slices of bread, toasted and cut into triangles

In a large pan, heat the oil and lightly sauté the leeks, onion, celery and carrots for approximately 4 minutes.

Add the chicken stock and let simmer over low heat for 15 minutes; season.

Add the tortellini and let simmer for another 10 minutes. In a bowl, beat the egg and add to the soup while stirring with a wooden spoon; cook for 1 minute.

Sprinkle with the parsley and basil. Pour into bowls and serve with freshly grated Parmesan and toasted bread.

CREAM OF ASPARAGUS SOUP

4 TO 6 SERVINGS

Preparation Time: 15 minutes

Cooking Time: 15 minutes

1 tbsp	(15 ml) butter
1/2 cup	(125 ml) coarsely chopped onion
1/2 cup	(125 ml) thinly sliced celery
1/2 cup	(125 ml) thinly sliced leeks
1 cup	(250 ml) chopped potatoes
12	asparagus spears cut into pieces
1 tbsp	(15 ml) chopped, fresh parsley
6 cups	(1.5 L) chicken stock
3/4 cup	(175 ml) 15% cream
	salt and pepper, to taste

GARNISH

red pepper coulis, store bought

In a saucepan, melt the butter and sauté the onions, celery, and leeks. Add the potatoes, asparagus, parsley, and chicken stock. Season and simmer for 20 to 25 minutes over low heat.

Purée the soup in a food processor, or by using an electric mixer. Return to the stove over low heat.

When ready to serve, incorporate the cream and garnish with the red pepper coulis.

RUOTE CHERVIL SOUP

4 SERVINGS

Preparation Time: 15 minutes

Cooking Time: 15 minutes

1	small onion
1	celery stalk
1	small white turnip
1 tsp	(5 ml) butter
4 cups	(1 L) chicken stock, skimmed of fat
2 cups	(500 ml) vegetable juice
	salt and pepper, to taste
1 1/2 cups	(375 ml) uncooked ruote (small wheel pasta)
2 tbsp	(25 ml) lime juice
1/4 cup	(50 ml) freshly chopped chervil or 1 tbsp (15 ml) dried chervil

GARNISH

1	green onion, sliced
4	small broccoli florets, cooked
4	small cauliflower florets, cooked

On a cutting board, chop the onion, cut the celery into thin slices and the turnip into small triangles; set aside.

In a saucepan, melt the butter and lightly sauté the onion, celery and turnip. Add the chicken stock and vegetable juice; season.

Let simmer over low heat for 5 minutes and add the ruote pasta; continue to cook for 10 minutes.

When ready to serve, add the lime juice and chervil. Garnish with green onion, clusters of broccoli and cauliflower florets.

ORRECHETTI ANTIPASTO SALAD

4 SERVINGS
Preparation Time: 15 minutes
Cooking Time: none

2 tsp	(10 ml) Dijon mustard
1	egg yolk
1/4 cup	(50 ml) olive oil
1 tbsp	(15 ml) red or white wine vinegar
1 tbsp	(15 ml) pesto
1 tbsp	(15 ml) spicy red pepper sauce, store bought
	salt and pepper, to taste
1/2 lb	(125 g) orrechetti pasta, cooked
1/2	red pepper, thinly sliced
1/2 cup	(125 ml) diced celery
1	green onion
1 1/2 cups	(375 ml) antipasto, store bought
1 tsp	(5 ml) paprika
2 tbsp	(25 ml) chopped, fresh parsley

GARNISH

endive leaves
cherry tomatoes
sprigs of parsley

In a large bowl, whisk together the Dijon mustard, the egg yolk, olive oil, vinegar, pesto and the red pepper sauce; season to taste.

Add the orrechetti pasta, red pepper, celery, green onion, antipasto, paprika and parsley; toss well.

Serve garnished with endive leaves, cherry tomatoes and sprigs of parsley.

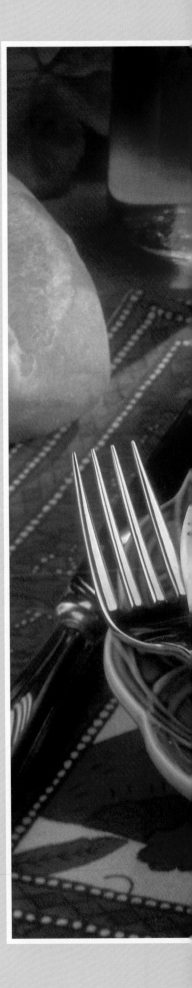

LOBSTER PASTA SALAD

4 SERVINGS

Preparation Time: 20 minutes

Cooking Time: 10 minutes

1/2 cup	(125 ml) olive oil
1/2 cup	(125 ml) sour cream
1/4 cup	(50 ml) lemon juice
1/2 cup	(125 ml) chopped fennel
1	small garlic clove, minced
2 cups	(500 ml) lobster meat, cooked and chopped
1 cup	(250 ml) diced tomatoes
2 tbsp	(25 ml) thinly sliced green onion
1 tsp	(5 ml) black pepper
1 cup	(250 g) fusilli pasta
	salt, to taste
1/4 cup	(50 ml) thinly sliced smoked salmon

In a large bowl, combine the oil, sour cream, lemon juice, fennel and garlic. Add the lobster, diced tomatoes, green onion and pepper. Mix well. Cover and let set at room temperature for 1 hour.

In the meantime, cook the pasta in boiling water for 8 to 10 minutes until tender. Drain the pasta and rinse with cold water. Drain again when the pasta has cooled.

Add the lobster mixture and the smoked salmon to the pasta. Toss well. Refrigerate for at least 1 hour before serving.

MUSSELS MARINARA

4 SERVINGS

Preparation Time: 15 minutes

Cooking Time: 5 minutes

4 lb	(2 kg) mussels, scrubbed and debearded
1/2 cup	(125 ml) dry white wine
1/2 cup	(5 ml) chopped green onions
1	stalk of celery, chopped
1	garlic clove, minced
1	pinch of thyme

Clean the mussels. In a large pot, mix together the wine, green onions, celery, garlic and thyme. Bring to a boil and add the mussels. Cover and cook over high heat for 3 to 5 minutes or until the mussels open. Discard any mussels that do not open.

Serve the cooked mussels in deep bowls. Pour the cooking juice over the mussels.

TUNA PESTO SALAD

4 SERVINGS

Preparation Time: 20 minutes

Cooking Time: none

PESTO

1 cup	(250 ml)	coarsely chopped, fresh basil
1 tbsp	(15 ml)	minced garlic
2 tbsp	(25 ml)	pine nuts
1/4 cup	(50 ml)	grated Parmesan cheese
1/2 cup	(125 ml)	olive oil

SALAD

2 tbsp	(25 ml)	Dijon mustard
1/4 cup	(50 ml)	mayonnaise
6 1/2 oz	(184 g)	2 cans of flaked tuna, drained
2		green onions, chopped
1 cup	(250 ml)	cubed tofu
1/2 cup	(125 ml)	diced celery
1 cup	(250 ml)	corn niblets
1		small red pepper, diced
12		green or black olives, pitted
		salt and pepper to taste
6		romaine lettuce leaves

GARNISH

8	anchovy filets
2	medium, hard-boiled eggs, cut into quarters
2	tomatoes, cut into quarters
4	sprigs of fresh basil

In a food processor, mix together all of the pesto ingredients. Incorporate the mustard and mayonnaise, mix lightly; set aside.

In a large bowl, mix together the tuna, onion, tofu, celery, corn niblets, red pepper and olives. Incorporate all of the pesto sauce and toss; season.

Line a serving platter or salad bowl with lettuce and add the tuna mix to the center.

Garnish with the anchovies, hard-boiled eggs, tomatoes, onion and sprigs of basil.

SUNNY PEACH SALAD

4 SERVINGS

Preparation Time: 15 minutes
Cooking Time: none

DRESSING

1/2 cup	(125 ml)	mayonnaise
1 tbsp	(15 ml)	Dijonnaise mustard
2 tbsp	(25 ml)	freshly squeezed lemon juice
		salt and pepper, to taste
4		peaches, peeled, pitted and sliced
1/2		avocado, peeled, pitted and sliced
14 oz	(398 ml)	mixed vegetables, drained
1		tomato, peeled and quartered
4		lettuce leaves

GARNISH

1/2 cup	(125 ml)	julienned carrots
4		sprigs of parsley (optional)

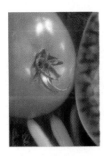

SAUCE

In a bowl, mix together the mayonnaise, Dijonnaise mustard and lemon juice; season.

In another bowl, combine the peaches, avocado, mixed vegetables and quartered tomatoes. Add the dressing and toss.

Line each plate with a lettuce leaf and the peach mixture. Garnish with julienned carrots and parsley to taste.

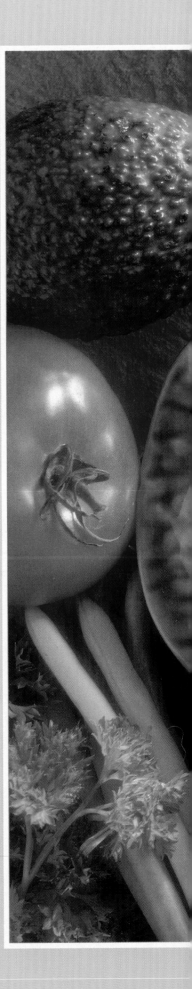

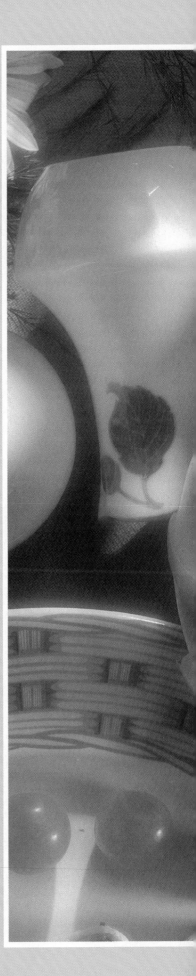
NICOISE SALAD

4 SERVINGS

Preparation Time: 25 minutes
Cooking Time: none

1	head of Boston lettuce
2 cups	(500 ml) green beans, blanched and cut into 1 in (2.5 cm) pieces
6 1/2 oz	(185 g) flaked tuna, drained
4	medium potatoes, cooked, cooled and diced
4	medium tomatoes, quartered
6	anchovy filets, rinsed and cut in half
2 tbsp	(25 ml) capers, drained

DRESSING

1 tbsp	(15 ml) Dijonnaise mustard
1 tbsp	(15 ml) mayonnaise
1/4 cup	(50 ml) white wine vinegar
1	garlic clove, minced
	salt and pepper, to taste
1/2 cup	(125 ml) olive oil

Tear the lettuce into bite-sized pieces and place on a large serving platter.

In a large bowl, mix together the green beans, tuna, potatoes and tomatoes. Place the mixture on top of the lettuce. Garnish with the anchovy filets, black olives and capers.

DRESSING

In a bowl or food processor, combine the Dijonnaise mustard, mayonnaise, vinegar and garlic; season and add olive oil.

Pour the dressing over the salad and serve.

QUICK CARBONARA PIZZA

4 SERVINGS

Preparation Time: 15 minutes
Cooking Time: 20 minutes

4	slices of crusty style Italian bread
1/2 lb	(250 g) bacon, cut into fine strips
2	small green onions, chopped
1 cup	(250 ml) 35% cream
2	tomatoes, seeded and sliced
1/2 cup	(125 ml) grated Parmesan cheese
1 tsp	(5 ml) dried oregano
1/2 tsp	(2 ml) crushed chili peppers
1 cup	(250 ml) grated mozzarella cheese
1	small green pepper, sliced

Preheat the oven to 400°F (200°C). Lightly toast the bread slices and set aside.

In a large pan, fry the bacon. When the bacon is crispy, add the onions. Drain the fat and add the cream, diced tomatoes, Parmesan cheese, oregano and chili peppers. Let simmer for 2 to 3 minutes so that the sauce thickens.

Spread the sauce onto the toasted bread. Garnish with mozzarella cheese and green pepper. Place on a cookie sheet and bake for 10 to 15 minutes until golden.

TOMATO AND BASIL PIZZA

4 SERVINGS

Preparation Time: 15 minutes
Cooking Time: 15 minutes

PIZZA DOUGH

2 tbsp	(25 ml) dry yeast
1 1/2 cups	(375 ml) warm water
4 cups	(1 L) all-purpose flour
1 tsp	(5 ml) salt
1 tsp	(5 ml) sugar
2 tbsp	(25 ml) olive oil

TOPPING

1 cup	(250 ml) olive oil
4 cups	(1 L) chopped, fresh basil or 2 tbsp (25 ml) dried basil
8	tomatoes, sliced
1/2 lb	(250 g) sliced ham or capicollo
1 lb	(500 g) grated mozzarella cheese

PIZZA DOUGH

In a bowl, combine the yeast and warm water, mix and let set for 6 minutes.

In an electric mixing bowl, mix together 3 cups (750 ml) of flour, salt and sugar. Add the yeast and olive oil; mix well. Slowly add 1 cup (250 ml) of flour until the dough becomes elastic but not sticky. Mold into a ball and place in a lightly oiled bowl. Cover with plastic wrap and let rise for 1 hour at room temperature.

Knead the dough and divide into 4 equal balls. On a countertop, roll out the dough to obtain 4 pizzas. Place on a baking sheet.

TOPPING

Preheat the oven to 400°F (200°C). In a bowl, mix together the olive oil and basil; set aside. Place the tomato slices on each pizza and drizzle the oil over. Cover with ham and cheese. Bake for 10 to 12 minutes and let brown under the broiler for 2 to 3 minutes. Serve.

PONTE VECCHIO PIZZA

4 SERVINGS

Preparation Time: 20 minutes
Cooking Time: 3 minutes

1/3 cup	(75 ml) olive oil
1/4 cup	(50 ml) chopped, fresh parsley
2 tsp	(10 ml) chopped, fresh oregano
2 tsp	(10 ml) chopped, fresh thyme
2 tbsp	(25 ml) chopped, fresh basil
	salt and pepper, to taste
1	green pepper, thinly sliced
1	red pepper, thinly sliced
1	red onion, thinly sliced
1	green zucchini, thinly sliced
1	yellow zucchini, thinly sliced
14 oz	(398 ml) artichoke hearts, drained and sliced
1/2 cup	(125 ml) sliced black olives
1/2 cup	(125 ml) sliced green olives
1 1/2 cups	(375 ml) sliced mushrooms
4	10 in. (25 cm) pizza pie dough
1 1/2 cups	(375 ml) tomato sauce, homemade or store bought
1 1/2 cups	(375 ml) grated Parmesan cheese

Preheat the oven to 400°F (200°C). In a large bowl, combine the olive oil with the parsley, oregano, thyme and basil; season.

Add all of the vegetables to the oil and herb mix; the green and red peppers, onion, green and yellow zucchini, artichokes, black and green olives, as well as the mushrooms. Mix well.

Spread the tomato sauce on the pizza pies and cover with the vegetable mixture. Sprinkle with Parmesan cheese.

Bake in the center of the oven for 10 minutes, and grill under the broiler for 3 minutes or until golden brown.

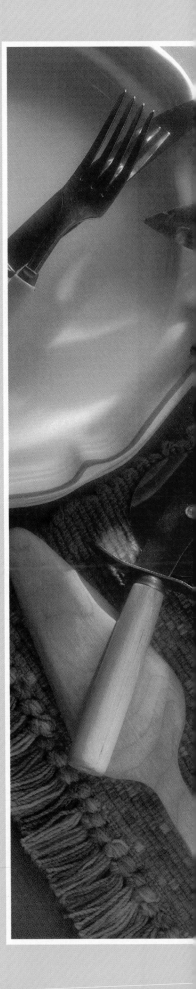

MEAT PIZZA

6 SERVINGS

Preparation Time: 15 minutes

Cooking Time: 35 to 40 minutes

3/4 lb	(375 g) lean ground veal
5	pork and beef sausages, casings removed and cut into small rounds
1 cup	(250 ml) bread crumbs
1	onion, sliced
1	medium egg, lightly beaten
1/3 cup	(75 ml) beef stock, skimmed of fat
1/2 tsp	(2 ml) garlic powder
3	drops of hot sauce
2 tbsp	(25 ml) chopped, fresh parsley
1	large pizza pie dough
1/2 cup	(125 ml) grated mozzerella cheese

Preheat the oven to 350°F (180°C). Cook the veal and sausages in a large, non-stick frying pan.

In a large bowl, combine the meat, breadcrumbs, onion, egg, beef stock, garlic powder, hot sauce and parsley; mix well.

Place the pizza dough on a 9 in (23 cm) baking sheet. Top with the meat mixture and sprinkle with cheese.

Bake for 35 to 40 minutes.

SEASONAL VEGETABLE PIZZA

4 SERVINGS

Preparation Time: 20 minutes

Cooking Time: 10 minutes

3	slices of bacon
1/2 cup	(125 ml) broccoli florets
1/2 cup	(125 ml) cauliflower florets
1 cup	(250 ml) mushrooms, quartered
2 tsp	(10 ml) butter
3 tbsp	(50 ml) butter
1/4 cup	(50 ml) all-purpose flour
2 cups	(500 ml) milk
1	pinch of ground nutmeg
1 cup	(250 ml) grated cheese, of choice
1	pizza dough, placed on a baking sheet

Preheat the oven to 400°F (200°C). Grill the bacon in the oven. Chop and set aside.

Cook the broccoli and cauliflower in salted, boiling water. Drain and set aside.

Sauté the mushrooms in 2 tsp (10 ml) of butter and set aside.

In a small saucepan, melt 3 tbsp (50 ml) of butter. Add the flour while mixing continuously. Add the milk and nutmeg. Let thicken and pour into a bowl; let cool.

When the mixture has cooled, spread onto the pizza dough. Top with the vegetables and sprinkle with cheese and bacon. Bake for 10 minutes and serve.

RED ONION AND GOAT CHEESE PIZZA

10 SERVINGS

Preparation Time: 30 minutes

Cooking Time: 25 to 30 minutes

CRUST

1 tsp	(5 ml) sugar or honey
1 1/4 cups	(300 ml) warm water
1	pinch of traditional dried yeast
3 cups	(750 ml) all-purpose flour
1 tsp	(5 ml) salt
2 tbsp	(25 ml) olive oil

TOPPING

3 tbsp	(50 ml) olive oil
3	red onions, chopped in thin rounds
1	garlic clove, minced
1/4 tsp	(1 ml) pepper
1/2 cup	(125 ml) grated Parmesan cheese
3/4 cup	(175 ml) black olives, cut in half
1/2 lb	(250 g) creamy goat cheese
2 tbsp	(25 ml) chopped, fresh basil or oregano
	chopped, fresh parsley, to taste

In a small bowl, dilute sugar or honey in 1/4 cup (50 ml) of warm water. Add the yeast and let set for 10 minutes or until the mixture becomes spongy.

In a large bowl, mix together 2 1/2 cups (625 ml) of flour and salt. In another bowl, mix the remaining warm water with the oil. Stir the yeast mixture and add it to the oil and water mixture. Add this mixture to the flour and salt preparation and mix until the dough has a soft texture. Add a sufficient amount of flour to obtain dough, which does not stick and is easy to separate.

Place the dough on a lightly floured surface and knead for 8 minutes or until it becomes smooth and elastic. Shape the dough into the form of a ball, place in a lightly greased bowl and turn to ensure the dough is completely greased. Cover with a cloth and let rise in a warm area for 1 hour or until the dough doubles in size.

In a pan, over medium-low heat, sauté the onions and garlic in oil for 5 minutes or until tender (do not burn). Pepper to taste.

Preheat the oven to 400°F (200°C). Knead and roll out the dough. Place on a baking sheet or a slightly greased pizza plate. Brush the dough with oil and sprinkle with Parmesan cheese.

Top with the onion mixture and olives. Sprinkle with goat cheese and season with basil or oregano and parsley.

Bake for 25 to 30 minutes until the crust is golden. Serve hot or cold.

VEGETABLE SPAGHETTI

4 SERVINGS

Preparation Time: 20 minutes
Cooking Time: 55 minutes

1	spaghetti squash, approximately 8 in (20 cm) in diameter
	sprigs of fresh herbs, of choice

SAUCE

1 tbsp	(15 ml) corn oil
2	garlic cloves, minced
28 oz	(796 ml) tomatoes with fine herbs
1 1/2 cups	(375 ml) sliced, fresh mushrooms
1 tsp	(5 ml) dry oregano
1 tsp	(5 ml) dry thyme
1 tbsp	(15 ml) sugar
	ground pepper, to taste

Cut the spaghetti squash in half and remove the seeds. Cover the squash with lightly oiled aluminum foil and bake at 350°F (180°C) for 30 to 45 minutes.

In the meantime, prepare the sauce. Heat the oil in a sauce pan and sauté the onions and garlic. Cook for 3 minutes. Add the tomatoes and bring to a boil. Add the mushrooms, oregano, thyme, sugar and pepper. Let simmer over low heat for 15 to 20 minutes.

With a fork, grate the interior of the squash to remove the flesh in spaghetti form. Place on a plate and cover with the tomato sauce. Garnish with fresh herbs and serve.

ZUCCHINI AND MUSHROOM FARFALLE

4 SERVINGS

Preparation Time: 15 minutes
Cooking Time: 15 minutes

2 tbsp	(25 ml) olive oil
2	green onions, sliced
1	zucchini, sliced in thin strips
1 1/2 cups	(375 ml) sliced mushrooms
	salt and pepper, to taste
1 tsp	(5 ml) minced garlic
2 tbsp	(25 ml) chopped, fresh parsley or 1 tsp (5 ml) dry parsley
2 tbsp	(25 ml) dry white wine (optional)
1 cup	(250 ml) chicken stock
10 oz	(284 ml) condensed cream of mushroom soup
1 cup	(250 ml) milk
1/2 lb	(250 g) cooked farfalle
	grated Parmesan cheese, to taste

In a pan, heat the olive oil and sauté the green onions, zucchini and mushrooms; season.

Add the garlic, parsley, white wine, chicken stock, cream of mushroom soup and milk. Let simmer over low heat for 5 minutes, or until desired consistency.

Serve the pasta onto plates. Pour the sauce over the pasta and sprinkle with Parmesan cheese.

CREAMY SPAGHETTI

2 SERVINGS

Preparation Time: 15 minutes

Cooking Time: 10 minutes

2 tsp	(10 ml) butter
1	shallot, chopped
10 to 12	mushrooms, sliced
1/4 cup	(50 ml) dry white wine
1 cup	(250 ml) creamy cheese sauce, store bought
1/4 cup	(50 ml) cream cheese
	salt and pepper to taste
7 oz	(200 g) cooked spaghetti
2 tbsp	(25 ml) chopped, fresh parsley

In a pan, melt the butter; add the shallots and sauté for 1 minute over medium heat.

Add the mushrooms and white wine. Cook until the liquid has completely evaporated. Add the creamy cheese sauce and cream cheese. Let thicken over low heat.

Season and add the spaghetti. Gently toss and garnish with parsley. Serve.

GERMELLI WITH CREAM OF MUSHROOM SAUCE

4 SERVINGS

Preparation Time: 15 minutes

Cooking Time: 20 minutes

2 tbsp	(25 ml) olive oil
2 tbsp	(25 ml) chopped shallots
1 1/2 cups	(375 ml) sliced mushrooms
1 cup	(250 ml) dry white wine
1/2 cup	(125 ml) chicken stock, skimmed of fat
1/2 cup	(125 ml) 35% cream
1/2 tsp	(2 ml) fresh chervil, chopped or dried
1 tsp	(5 ml) melted butter
1 tsp	(5 ml) all-purpose flour salt and pepper, to taste
6 oz	(180 g) germelli or penne pasta, cooked and hot

GARNISH

1	tomato, seeded and diced
4	sprigs of chervil or fresh parsley

In a pan, heat the oil and sauté the shallots. Add the mushrooms and cook for 2 to 3 minutes over medium heat. Add the white wine and chicken stock and reduce by half.

Add the cream and chervil. Thicken with a mixture of butter and flour; season. Purée in a food processor or by using an electric mixer. Return to the pan and heat.

Remove from the stove and add the pasta. Toss well and serve garnished with tomatoes and chervil.

TAGLIATELLE WITH GARLIC SAUCE

4 SERVINGS

Preparation Time: 15 minutes

Cooking Time: 35 minutes

1 tbsp (15 ml) butter
1 tbsp (15 ml) corn oil
2 onions, chopped
6 garlic cloves, minced
1 tbsp (15 ml) all-purpose flour
1/4 cup (50 ml) chicken stock, skimmed of fat
pepper, to taste
1 lb (500 g) tagliatelle pasta, cooked and hot
1/3 cup (75 ml) grated Sbrinz cheese

In a pan, melt the butter and add the oil. Sauté the onions and garlic for 5 minutes. Add the flour, chicken stock and pepper. Mix well. Cover and let simmer for 30 minutes over very low heat.

Purée in a food processor until the sauce becomes smooth and creamy. Transfer to a big serving bowl.

Add the pasta and cheese to the sauce. Toss well and serve.

FLORENTINE TORTELLINI

4 SERVINGS

Preparation Time: 15 minutes

Cooking Time: 20 minutes

1 tbsp (15 ml) corn oil
1/4 cup (50 ml) chopped onions
1 tsp (5 ml) minced garlic
28 oz (796 ml) crushed tomatoes with fine herbs
salt and pepper, to taste
10 oz (284 ml) condensed cream of mushroom soup
1 tbsp (15 ml) butter
1 package of fresh spinach
1/2 lb (250 g) tortellini pasta, cooked and hot
1 tbsp (15 ml) chopped, fresh parsley

In a large pan, heat the oil and sauté the onions. Add the garlic and tomatoes; season. Let simmer for 10 minutes over low heat.

Add the cream of mushroom soup and cook over low heat, set aside and keep warm.

In a pan, melt the butter and add the spinach. Lightly cook for 1 minute. Mix with the pasta.

Serve with sauce and garnish with parsley.

FETTUCCINI IN CREAMY ENDIVE SAUCE

4 SERVINGS

Preparation Time: 15 minutes

Cooking Time: 15 minutes

2 tbsp	(25 ml) olive oil
4	endives, coarsely chopped
2	green onions, sliced
3/4 cup	(175 ml) sliced celery
	salt and pepper, to taste
1 cup	(250 ml) chicken stock
10 oz	(284 ml) condensed cream of chicken soup
1 cup	(250 ml) 15% cream
2 tbsp	(25 ml) chopped, fresh parsley or 1 tsp (5 ml) dry parsley
1/4 cup	(50 ml) grated Parmesan cheese
1/2 cup	(250 g) fettuccini pasta, cooked and hot

GARNISH

12	snow peas, blanched
6	sundried tomatoes, sliced
	endive leaves
	cherry tomatoes
	sprig of parsley, to taste

In a pan, heat the olive oil and sauté the endives, celery and green onions. Add the chicken stock; season, cover and let simmer over low heat. Purée in a food processor or with an electric mixer. Return to the pan, add the cream  of chicken soup, cream, and parsley. Let simmer for 2 to 3 minutes and add the fettuccini.

Sprinkle with Parmesan cheese and serve on plates garnished with snowpeas, sundried tomatoes, endive leaves and parsley.

VEAL FLORENTINE

4 SERVINGS

Preparation Time: 20 minutes
Cooking Time: 15 to 20 minutes

2	eggs
1/2 cup	(125 ml) milk
4	slices of white or whole wheat bread, crusts removed
4	veal scallops
4	slices of Mozzarella cheese or 1 cup (250 ml) grated mozzarella
12	spinach leaves, blanched
1 tsp	(5 ml) dried basil
1 tsp	(5 ml) dried oregano
	salt and pepper, to taste
1 tbsp	(15 ml) olive oil
2	small green onions, chopped
1 tsp	(5 ml) minced garlic
2	tomatoes, seeded and diced
1 1/2 cups	(375 ml) white wine or chicken stock

In a large bowl, mix together the eggs and milk. On a countertop, use a rolling pin to flatten the bread. Dip the bread in the mixture of eggs and milk.

Garnish each veal scallop with a slice of bread, a slice of cheese and spinach. Sprinkle with basil and oregano. Season and roll up tightly. Secure with string or a toothpick.

In a pan, heat the oil and braise the veal. Set aside and keep warm.

Add the onions, garlic and tomatoes to the pan. Heat and add the wine; let reduce.

Cut the veal rolls into thin slices. Serve on plates covered with the cooking broth.

VEAL À LA DIJON

4 SERVINGS

Preparation Time: 15 minutes
Cooking Time: 15 minutes

8	veal scallops 3 oz (90 g) each
2 tsp	(10 ml) corn oil
1 tsp	(5 ml) butter
	salt and pepper, to taste
2	shallots, chopped
1	small cluster of fine herbs (1 sprig of thyme, 1 bay leaf, 1 sprig of parsley)
1/2 cup	(125 ml) dry white wine (optional)
1/2 cup	(125 ml) chicken stock, skimmed of fat
2 tbsp	(25 ml) Dijon mustard
1/2 cup	(125 ml) 35% cream or chicken stock, skimmed of fat
1 tsp	(5 ml) brown sauce thickener
1/2 lb	(250 g) fettuccini pasta, cooked and hot
2 tbsp	(25 ml) chopped, fresh parsley

On a cutting board, flatten the veal scallops.

In a pan, heat the oil, and melt the butter by gradually increasing the heat; season. Cook the veal for 1 minute on each side.

Remove the veal from the pan and keep warm. Add the shallots and the cluster of herbs. Add the white wine and the chicken stock; reduce by half.

Add the mustard and cream; let simmer for 2 minutes. Thicken with brown sauce and strain. Set aside and keep warm.

Serve the veal on a platter and cover with sauce. Accompany with fettuccini garnished with parsley.

SLICED VEAL

4 SERVINGS

Preparation Time: 20 minutes
Cooking Time: 15 to 20 minutes

20 oz	(600 g) veal scallops, cut into thin strips
1/3 cup	(75 ml) all-purpose flour pepper to taste
1/4 cup	(50 ml) butter
1/4 cup	(50 ml) finely chopped onion
2/3 cup	(150 ml) sliced fresh mushrooms
1/3 cup	(75 ml) white wine or dry white Vermouth
1/2 cup	(125 ml) 35 % cream
1/4 tsp	(1 ml) paprika
GARNISH	
	parsley, to taste

Mix the flour and pepper on a plate and lightly coat the strips of veal, removing any excess flour.

Place the veal in a non-stick pan, with 1/3 cup (75 ml) of butter, and cook over medium heat for 7 to 10 minutes, turning frequently.

Remove from the stove, place on a plate, and keep warm.

Melt the remaining butter in a pan and add the onion. Cook over medium heat, while stirring frequently with a wooden spoon. Add the mushrooms and cook over medium heat for 2 minutes, stirring continuously. Add the white wine and bring to a boil.

Reduce the heat and let simmer for approximately 1 minute, add the cream, paprika and veal strips. Cook for 4 to 5 minutes.

Serve on warmed plates and garnish with parsley. Accompany with pasta.

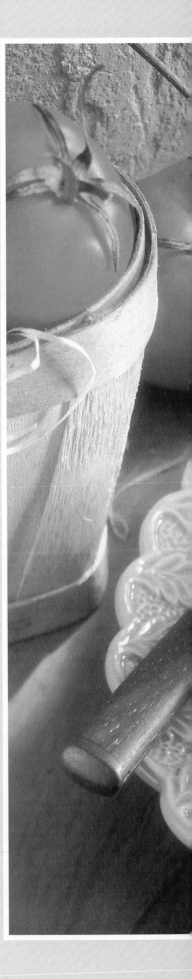

MAFALDINNE VEAL STEW

4 TO 6 SERVINGS
Preparation Time: 20 minutes
Cooking Time: 2 hours

1 tbsp	(15 ml)	olive oil
1 1/2 lb	(780 g)	veal, cubed
2 tbsp	(25 ml)	chopped shallots
1 tsp	(5 ml)	minced garlic
1 tsp	(5 ml)	ground cumin
1 tsp	(5 ml)	dried oregano
1 cup	(250 ml)	dry white wine (optional)
2 cups	(500 ml)	chicken stock, skimmed of fat
28 oz	(796 ml)	crushed tomatoes with fine herbs
		salt and pepper, to taste
1 tbsp	(15 ml)	butter
1 tbsp	(15 ml)	all-purpose flour
1 tbsp	(15 ml)	olive oil
3/4 lb	(375 g)	hot, cooked, mafaldinne pasta (or lasagnette)
2		green onions, sliced
		salt and pepper, to taste
1 tsp	(5 ml)	minced garlic
1 tbsp	(15 ml)	grated Parmesan cheese
1 tsp	(5 ml)	chopped, fresh parsley

GARNISH

black or green olives
sprig of parsley

In a pan, heat the oil and brown the veal over high heat. Add the shallots and continue cooking for 1 to 2 minutes. Add the garlic, cumin and oregano.

Add the white wine, chicken stock and tomatoes. Cover and let simmer for 1 hour 30 minutes over low heat. Season and thicken the sauce with a mixture of butter and flour; set aside.

In a large pan or pot, heat the oil. Sauté the pasta and green onions; season. Add the garlic, cheese and parsley. Place the pasta on plates and top with the veal stew. Garnish with olives and a sprig of parsley.

VEAL DE LA CASA

4 SERVINGS

Preparation Time: 20 minutes
Cooking Time: 1 hour 15 minutes

1/4 cup	(50 ml) olive oil
1 tbsp	(15 ml) minced garlic
1 cup	(250 ml) chopped, fresh basil or 1 tbsp (15 ml) dry basil
1/4	bag of spinach, cut into small pieces, washed and cooked
1/4 cup	(50 ml) grated Parmesan cheese
8	veal scallops, well flattened
1 tbsp	(15 ml) olive oil
2 tbsp	(25 ml) chopped shallots
1 tbsp	(15 ml) minced garlic
28 oz	(796 ml) tomatoes, peeled and crushed
1 cup	(250 ml) tomato juice
2 cups	(500 ml) beef stock, skimmed of fat
2 tbsp	(25 ml) chopped, fresh basil or 1/2 tsp (2 ml) dry basil
2	sprigs of fresh oregano or 1 tsp (2 ml) dry oregano
2	bay leaves
	salt and pepper, to taste
1 tbsp	(15 ml) cornstarch, diluted in a bit of water
1/2 cup	(125 ml) 35% cream (optional)
3/4 lb	(375 g) curly pasta, cooked and hot (fusilli pasta)
12	black olives
4	sprigs of fresh basil
2 tbsp	(25 ml) grated Parmesan cheese

In a bowl, mix together the olive oil, garlic, basil, spinach and Parmesan cheese. Spread this mixture on the veal scallops and roll up. Secure with a string or toothpick.

In a pan, heat the olive oil and sear each side of the veal. Remove the veal from the pan and set aside.

Add the shallots and sauté lightly. Add the garlic, tomatoes, tomato juice, beef stock, basil, oregano, and bay leaves. Season and let simmer for 1 hour over low heat.

Thicken the sauce with cornstarch and add the cream. Serve the veal on top of the pasta and cover with the sauce. Garnish with black olives, a sprig of basil and Parmesan cheese.

ANGEL HAIR PASTA WITH MEAT SAUCE

4 SERVINGS

Preparation Time: 20 minutes
Cooking Time: 30 minutes

2 tbsp	(25 ml) olive oil
4 oz	(120 g) cooked ham, diced
4 oz	(120 g) Italian sausages, blanched and sliced
4 oz	(120 g) smoked turkey, cut into thin strips
2	green onions, sliced
2 tsp	(10 ml) minced garlic
28 oz	(796 ml) tomatoes with fine herbs, peeled and crushed
1	bay leaf
1 1/2 cups	(375 ml) veal stock or beef stock, skimmed of fat
	salt and pepper, to taste
1 tbsp	(15 ml) cornstarch diluted in a bit of water
1/2 cup	(125 ml) 15% cream
1/2 lb	(250 g) angel hair pasta, cooked and hot
2 cups	(500 ml) hot vegetables, blanched and cut into sticks
1/2 cup	(125 ml) grated Parmesan cheese
2 tbsp	(25 ml) chopped, fresh parsley

In a pan, heat the olive oil and lightly brown the ham, sausages, smoked turkey and green onions.

Add the garlic, tomatoes, bay leaf, and stock. Season and let simmer over low heat for 20 minutes.

Thicken the sauce with cornstarch and incorporate the cream when ready to serve.

Place the pasta on four plates and cover with sauce. Top with vegetables; garnish with cheese and parsley.

FUSILLI WITH RICOTTA SAUCE

4 SERVINGS

Preparation Time: 15 minutes
Cooking Time: 20 minutes

1/2 cup	(125 ml) dry white wine or unsweetened apple juice
2 tbsp	(25 ml) chicken stock, skimmed of fat
1 1/2 cups	(375 ml) 15% cream
3/4 cup	(175 ml) ham, cut into thin strips
1 cup	(250 ml) ricotta cheese
14 oz	(400 g) cooked, hot fusilli pasta

In a small pan, combine the wine or apple juice and chicken stock. Cook over medium heat and reduce by half.

Add the cream and reduce by 1/3.

Add 2/3 of the ham and the cheese, mix delicately and keep warm.

Toss the fusilli with the sauce. Place on the plates and garnish with the remaining ham.

FUSILLI WITH HAM AND ZUCCHINI

4 SERVINGS

Preparation Time: 15 minutes
Cooking Time: 25 minutes

2 tbsp (25 ml) olive oil
2 zucchini, cut in half-rounds
1/2 cup (125 ml) cooked ham,
cut into strips
1/2 lb (375 g) fusilli, cooked and hot

TOMATO SAUCE

2 tbsp (25 ml) olive oil
2 tbsp (25 ml) chopped shallots
1/2 cup (125 ml) diced celery
1/2 cup (125 ml) diced carrots
1 tbsp (15 ml) minced garlic
28 oz (796 ml) tomatoes,
peeled and crushed
1 cup (250 ml) beef stock
salt and pepper, to taste
1 tbsp (15 ml) cornstarch diluted
in water

TOMATO SAUCE

In a large saucepan, heat the olive oil and lightly brown the shallots, celery and carrots. Add the garlic, tomatoes, and beef stock; season and let simmer for 15 to 20 minutes over low heat. Mix with cornstarch and keep warm.

In a large pan, heat the oil and brown the zucchini for 1 to 2 minutes over high heat. Add the ham, fusilli and tomato sauce; heat and serve.

PANCETTA HAM LINGUINI

4 SERVINGS

Preparation Time: 10 minutes
Cooking Time: 10 minutes

2 tbsp (25 ml) olive oil
1 green onion, chopped
1 red or green pepper, diced
6 oz (180 g) diced Pancetta ham
2 tomatoes, seeded and diced
1/4 cup (50 ml) pesto
2 tbsp (25 ml) chopped, fresh parsley
1/4 lb (125 g) whole wheat linguini,
cooked and hot
1/4 lb (125 g) spinach linguini,
cooked and hot
salt and pepper, to taste
grated Parmesan cheese, to taste

In a large pan or casserole, heat the olive oil and sauté the green onions and the pepper with the Pancetta ham. Add the diced tomatoes, pesto, parsley and linguini. Toss and season.

Garnish with grated Parmesan cheese and serve.

LINGUINI WITH ARTICHOKES

4 SERVINGS

Preparation Time: 15 minutes

Cooking Time: 7 minutes

1 tbsp	(15 ml) olive oil
2	garlic cloves, minced
1 1/4 cups	(300 ml) Pancetta ham, cut into thin strips
14 oz	(398 ml) artichokes, drained and cut in 4
1/4 cup	(50 ml) dry white wine
2 cups	(500 ml) chopped, fresh spinach
1 lb	(500 g) linguini pasta, hot and cooked
	salt and pepper, to taste
1 cup	(250 ml) chopped bocconcini cheese

In a pan, heat the oil over medium heat and add the garlic. Sauté for 1 minute. Add the Pancetta ham and let cook for 1 minute.

Add the artichokes, white wine and spinach. Cook for 1 minute or until the spinach is cooked.

Add the linguini, season and toss.

Serve on warm plates and garnish with bocconcini cheese.

GNOCCHI WITH HAM

4 SERVINGS

Preparation Time: 10 minutes
Cooking Time: 15 minutes

1 tbsp	(15 ml) olive oil
2 tbsp	(25 ml) chopped shallots
2 tsp	(10 ml) minced garlic
4 oz	(125 g) ham or capicollo cut into thin strips
1 cup	(250 g) chicken stock
28 oz	(756 ml) tomatoes, peeled and diced
	salt and pepper, to taste
1 tbsp	(15 ml) cornstarch diluted in a bit of water
1 tbsp	(15 ml) pesto
1/2 cup	(125 ml) 15% cream (optional)
4	sprigs of basil or parsley
1/2 lb	(250 g) gnocchi pasta, cooked and hot

In a large pan, heat the oil and sauté the shallots. Add the garlic, ham, chicken stock, and tomatoes. Season and let simmer over low heat for 10 minutes.

Thicken with the cornstarch, and add the pesto and cream. Place the pasta on plates, add the sauce and garnish with basil.

When serving, sprinkle with Parmesan cheese.

BACON AND RICOTTA LASAGNA

4 SERVINGS

Preparation Time: 20 minutes
Cooking Time: 40 minutes

2 tbsp	(25 ml)	olive oil
3/4 cup	(175 ml)	chopped onion
1 tbsp	(15 ml)	minced garlic
28 oz	(796 ml)	tomatoes, peeled and crushed
1 tsp	(5 ml)	dried basil
1 tsp	(5 ml)	dried oregano
1		bay leaf
1		sprig of thyme
1		sprig of parsley
1 tbsp	(15 ml)	cornstarch, diluted in a bit of water
1/2 lb	(250 g)	lasagna pasta, cooked and hot
2 cups	(500 ml)	ricotta cheese
1/2 lb	(250 g)	bacon, cooked and chopped
1/4 lb	(125 g)	thin strips of capicollo
2 cups	(500 ml)	grated mozzarella cheese

In a pan, heat the oil and sauté the onions. Add the garlic and mix with the tomatoes.

Add the basil, oregano, and cluster of spices. Let simmer over medium heat for 20 minutes. Thicken with cornstarch.

Preheat the oven to 375°F (190°C). Cover the bottom of a baking dish with a bit of sauce. Place a layer of lasagna strips in the dish. Spread another layer (1/3) of sauce. Sprinkle with half of the ricotta cheese, the bacon and capicollo. Repeat once more and finish with a layer of lasagna strips and sauce. Sprinkle with mozzarella cheese.

Bake for 30 to 35 minutes or until the cheese is golden brown.

GOURMET RICOTTA SPAGHETTI

4 SERVINGS

Preparation Time: 15 minutes

Cooking Time: 20 minutes

2 tbsp	(25 ml) olive oil
2	green onions, sliced
1 cup	(250 ml) sliced mushrooms
1	red pepper, chopped
6 oz	(180 g) cooked ham, cut in thin strips
1 tbsp	(15 ml) minced garlic
1 tbsp	(15 ml) chopped, fresh parsley
3 cups	(75 ml) chicken stock, skimmed of fat
1/2 cup	(125 ml) 35% cream
2 tbsp	(25 ml) all-purpose flour
2 tbsp	(25 ml) melted butter salt and pepper, to taste
1 cup	(250 ml) ricotta cheese spaghetti, cooked and hot
3/4 lb	(375 g) grated Parmesan cheese

In a large pan, heat the oil and sauté the onions, mushrooms, peppers and ham.

Add the garlic and chicken stock. Let simmer for 5 minutes over medium heat and add the cream. Thicken the sauce with a mixture of flour and butter (add slowly until desired consistency is obtained); season to taste.

When ready to serve, add the ricotta cheese. Cover the pasta with sauce and sprinkle with Parmesan cheese.

HAM AND SPINACH LASAGNA

4 TO 6 SERVINGS

Preparation Time: 15 minutes

Cooking Time: 20 minutes

2 tbsp	(25 ml) butter
2 tbsp	(25 ml) all-purpose flour
2 cups	(500 ml) hot milk
2 1/2 cups	(625 ml) tomato sauce
1/2 lb	(250 g) thin strips of cooked ham
1	bag of spinach, washed and blanched
1	box of pre-cooked lasagna
1 cup	(250 ml) ricotta cheese (optional)
1 1/2 cups	(375 ml) grated mozzarella cheese

In a pan, melt the butter, add the flour and mix well. Add the milk and cook over low heat for 10 minutes; season.

Add the ham, tomato sauce and spinach. Preheat the oven to 350°F (180°C). Pour 1/3 cup (75 ml) of the sauce into a greased baking pan. Place the first layer of lasagna over the sauce; cover with a second layer of lasagna, sauce and ricotta cheese.

Repeat until the ninth layer of lasagna is covered with sauce. Cover with aluminum foil and bake for 15 minutes. Remove the aluminum foil, sprinkle with mozzarella cheese and finish cooking under the broiler.

SPAGHETTI WITH TOMATO SAUCE

4 SERVINGS

Preparation Time: 10 minutes

Cooking Time: 15 minutes

2 tbsp	(25 ml) olive oil
3/4 cup	(175 ml) chopped onion
1	small green pepper, sliced
1	small red pepper, sliced
1 tsp	(5 ml) minced garlic
28 oz	(750 ml) crushed tomatoes with fine herbs
1/2 lb	(250 g) spaghetti, cooked and hot
1/2 cup	(125 g) grated Parmesan cheese
1/2 lb	(250 g) cooked bacon, chopped
	salt and pepper, to taste

In a saucepan, heat the olive oil. Sauté the onion and peppers. Add the garlic and tomatoes. Let simmer over low heat for 10 minutes. Add the pasta, Parmesan cheese and bacon. Season and mix well.

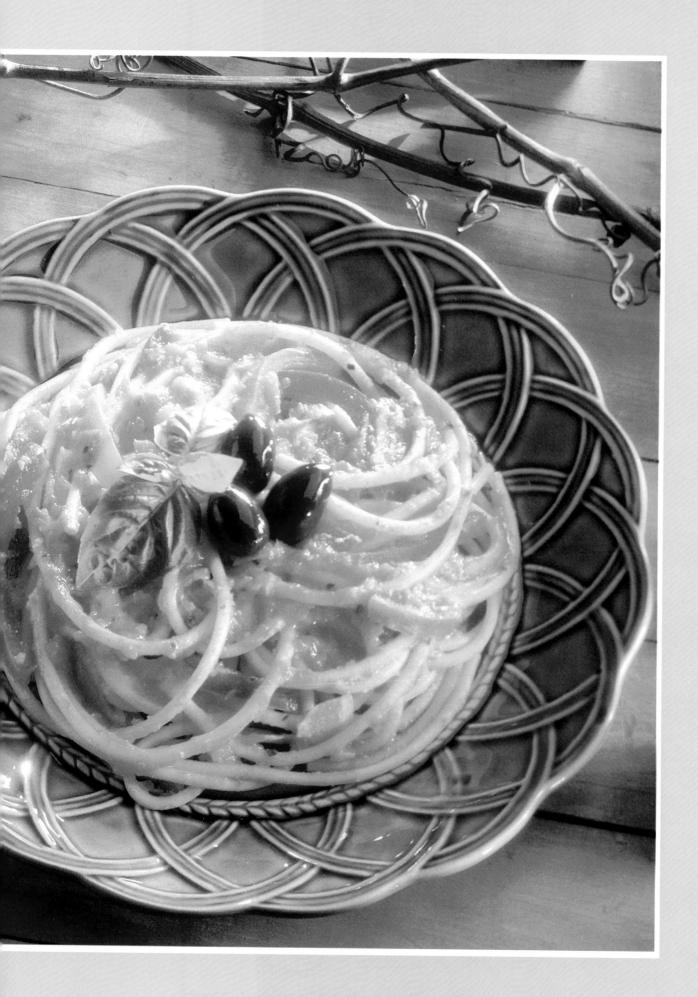

GERMELLI WITH CHICKEN

4 TO 6 SERVINGS

Preparation Time: 20 minutes
Cooking Time: 35 minutes

ROSÉ SAUCE

2 tbsp	(25 ml) olive oil
2 tbsp	(25 ml) chopped shallots
2 tbsp	(25 ml) minced garlic
1 cup	(250 ml) dry white wine (optional)
28 oz	(796 ml) tomatoes, peeled and crushed
1 1/2 cups	(375 ml) veal or beef stock
1 tsp	(5 ml) dried oregano
1 tsp	(5 ml) dried basil
1	bay leaf
1	sprig of thyme
1	sprig of parsley
	salt and pepper, to taste
1 tbsp	(15 ml) cornstarch diluted in water
1/2 cup	(125 ml) 35% cream
1/2 lb	(375 ml) germelli pasta, cooked and hot

CHICKEN

1 tbsp	(15 ml) olive oil
1 lb	(500 ml) chicken breasts, cut into strips
	salt and pepper, to taste
16	blanched snowpeas
1 box	(199 ml) water chestnuts, cut into round slices
1 1/2 cups	(375 ml) chopped carrots
1/2	red pepper, sliced
1/4 cup	(50 ml) grated Parmesan cheese
2 tbsp	(25 ml) chopped, fresh parsley

ROSÉ SAUCE

In a pan, heat the oil and sauté the shallots. Add the garlic, white wine, tomatoes, veal stock, oregano, basil and spices; season.

Cover and let simmer over low heat for 25 minutes. Remove the bay leaf and thicken the sauce with cornstarch. When ready to serve, incorporate the cream and the pasta.

CHICKEN

In a large pan, heat the oil and brown the chicken strips for 2 to 3 minutes or longer if desired. Season to taste. Add the snowpeas, water chestnuts, carrots, and red pepper; cook over low heat.

Serve the germelli pasta garnished with the chicken. Sprinkle with Parmesan cheese and chopped parsley.

PENNE WITH CHICKEN

4 SERVINGS

Preparation Time: 10 minutes
Cooking Time: 20 minutes

2	boneless, skinless, chicken breasts, cut into strips
1 1/2 cups	(375 ml) small broccoli florets
3 tbsp	(50 ml) olive oil
1/4 cup	(50 ml) butter
1/4 cup	(50 ml) all-purpose flour
1 tsp	(5 ml) dry mustard
2 cups	(500 ml) milk
1 1/2 cups	(375 ml) grated cheddar cheese
1 lb	(500 g) penne pasta, cooked
1	pinch of salt
	ground pepper, to taste

Sauté the chicken strips and broccoli in olive oil until the chicken is lightly browned.

In a pan, melt the butter over low heat. Incorporate the flour and dry mustard, while mixing continuously. Slowly stir in the milk until the mixture thickens. It should become creamy.

Add the cheese and let it melt. Add the mixture of chicken and broccoli to the pasta and season. Serve very hot.

FETTUCCINI WITH TURKEY AND SUNDRIED TOMATO SAUCE

4 SERVINGS

Preparation Time: 20 minutes
Cooking Time: 45 minutes

1 tbsp	(15 ml) butter
1 lb	(500 g) turkey breast, boneless and cut into pieces
	salt and pepper, to taste
1	bay leaf
1	sprig of parsley
1	sprig of thyme
2 cups	(500 ml) chicken stock
1 cup	(250 ml) dry white wine
1 tbsp	(15 ml) butter
1 tbsp	(15 ml) all-purpose flour
1 cup	(250 ml) 15% cream
1/2 lb	(250 g) fettuccini pasta
1/2 cup	(125 ml) sundried tomato sauce (store bought)
2 tbsp	(25 ml) chopped, fresh basil or parsley

Cook the fettuccini according to the directions on the package.

In a pan, melt the butter and cook the turkey until golden; season. Add the spices, chicken stock and white wine. Let simmer over low heat for 30 minutes. Stir in the mixture of butter and flour. Let simmer until the sauce thickens. Add the cream and bring to a boil.

Serve the turkey over the fettuccini with a bit of the sundried tomato sauce in the middle. Sprinkle with parsley or basil.

LINGUINI WITH TURKEY

4 SERVINGS

Preparation Time: 20 minutes
Cooking Time: 15-20 minutes

	salt and pepper, to taste
1/4 cup	(50 ml) all-purpose flour
3/4 lb	(375 g) smoked turkey, cut into strips
1 tbsp	(15 ml) butter
1 tbsp	(15 ml) canola oil
2 tbsp	(25 ml) cognac or brandy
1/2 cup	(125 ml) grilled and chopped hazelnuts
1 cup	(250 ml) 15% cream
1 lb	(500 g) cooked linguini
1	pinch of nutmeg

Season and lightly coat the turkey strips with flour. In a pan, heat the butter and oil over medium high heat and sauté the turkey until lightly golden. Remove from the pan and set aside.

Pour the brandy or cognac into the pan, add the nuts and cream. Heat for 5 to 7 minutes or until the sauce slightly thickens. Place the strips of meat back into the pan and let simmer over low heat for 5 minutes.

Season the hot linguini with nutmeg and place on the plates; cover with sauce.

PENNE IN A CREAM SAUCE WITH CHICKEN

4 SERVINGS

Preparation Time: 15 minutes

Cooking Time: 30 minutes

1 tbsp	(15 ml) olive oil
1 lb	(500 g) chicken breast, flattened and cut into thin strips
2	green onions, sliced
4 oz	(125 g) prosciutto or capicollo
1 tsp	(5 ml) minced garlic
1	bay leaf
1	sprig of parsley
1	sprig of thyme
12 oz	(341 ml) beer
28 oz	(796 ml) tomatoes with fine herbs, peeled and crushed
1 cup	(250 ml) beef stock, skimmed of fat
	salt and pepper, to taste
1 tbsp	(15 ml) cornstarch diluted in water
1/2 cup	(125 ml) 15% cream
1/2 lb	(375 g) cooked penne pasta, hot
	cooked vegetables, of choice
1/2 cup	(125 ml) grated Parmesan cheese

In a pan, heat the oil and brown the chicken strips; add the green onions and prosciutto or capicollo. Incorporate the garlic and spices.

Add the beer, tomatoes, and beef stock; season. Remove the chicken and set aside, keeping it warm. Continue to cook the sauce over low heat for 20 to 25 minutes. Thicken with cornstarch and return the chicken to the sauce.

When ready to serve, incorporate the cream. Place the chicken strips on the plates, accompany with penne and sprinkle with fine herbs, a few vegetables and Parmesan cheese.

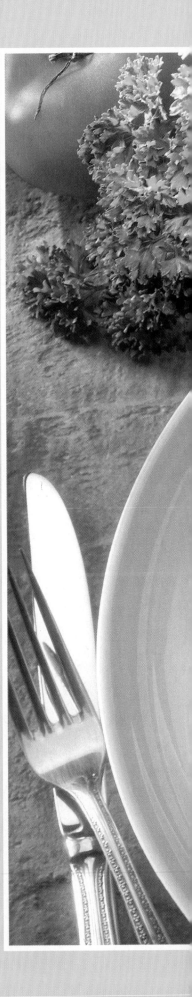

SEAFOOD TAGLIATELLE

4 SERVINGS

Preparation Time: 20 minutes

Cooking Time: 20 minutes

SEAFOOD SAUCE

1 tbsp	(15 m) olive oil
2 tbsp	(25 ml) chopped shallots
16	mussels, scrubbed and debearded
16	jumbo shrimp, cleaned and deveined
16	scallops
2 tbsp	(25 ml) chopped, fresh parsley
	salt and pepper, to taste
1 cup	(250 ml) dry white wine or chicken stock
1 cup	(250 ml) fish stock or chicken stock
2 tbsp	(25 ml) melted butter
2 tbsp	(25 ml) all-purpose flour
1/2 cup	(125 ml) 35% cream
4 oz	(125 g) crab or lobster meat (optional)
4 cups	(1 L) salted boiling water
	tagliatelle pasta
	fine herbs, of choice

In a pan, heat the olive oil and sauté the shallots. Add the shrimp, scallops, mussels and parsley. Season and cook for 1 to 2 minutes. Add the white wine, cover and let simmer for 1 to 2 minutes until the mussels open.

Remove the seafood and set aside; add the fish stock and bring to a boil. Add a mixture of butter and flour. Incorporate the cream, mussels, shrimp, scallops and crab. Set aside and keep warm.

TAGLIATELLE

In a large pan, bring the water to a boil. Cook the tagliatelle by following the instructions on the package. Drain well and serve.

Serve the pasta on 4 plates, cover with the seafood sauce and garnish with fine herbs.

TUTTOMARE LINGUINI

4 SERVINGS
Preparation Time: 25 minutes
Cooking Time: 15 minutes

2 tbsp	(25 ml) oil
3	garlic cloves, minced
1 cup	(250 ml) chopped mushrooms
1	pinch of cayenne pepper
1/4 cup	(50 ml) brandy
1/2 cup	(125 ml) dry white wine
1 cup	(250 ml) tomato sauce, store bought
4 1/2 oz	(142 g) clams, in their juice
	salt and pepper, to taste
20	mussels, scrubbed and debearded
1/2 lb	(250 g) haddock filet cut into 1 in (2.5 cm) pieces
1/2 lb	(250 g) small shrimp, shelled and raw
1/2 lb	(250 g) scallops
1 lb	(500 g) linguini, cooked and hot
2 tbsp	(25 ml) finely chopped, fresh basil

In a pan, heat the oil over medium-high heat. Add the garlic, mushrooms and cayenne pepper; cook for 3 minutes. Add the brandy, let it evaporate and add the white wine, tomato sauce and clam juice. Let simmer for 3 minutes; season.

Add the clams, mussels, haddock, shrimp and scallops. Cover and let simmer for 6 to 8 minutes or until the mussels open.

Place the pasta on plates and cover with seafood sauce. Sprinkle with basil and serve.

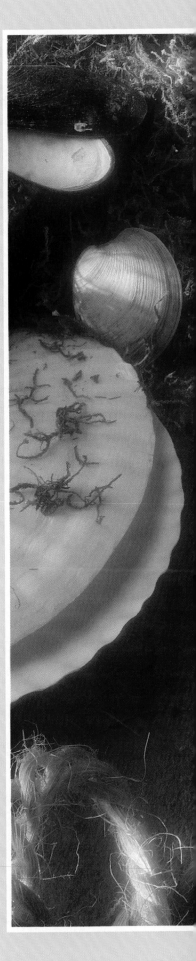

SPAGHETTINI WITH MUSHROOMS AND ANCHOVIES

4 SERVINGS
Preparation Time: 15 minutes
Cooking Time: 15 minutes

2 tbsp	(25 ml) butter
2 cups	(500 ml) sliced mushrooms
8	filets of anchovy, rinsed in water and sliced
1/4 cup	(50 ml) dry white wine
1 cup	(250 ml) chicken stock, skimmed of fat
	ground pepper, to taste
2 cups	(500 ml) milk
2 tbsp	(25 ml) potato starch
2 tbsp	(25 ml) Dijonnaise mustard
1 lb	(500 g) spaghettini, cooked and hot
2 tbsp	(25 ml) chopped, fresh parsley
1/4 cup	(50 ml) grated Parmesan cheese

GARNISH

4 anchovy filets, rinsed in water and cut in half.

In a pan, melt the butter and cook the mushrooms and anchovies for 3 minutes. Add the white wine and chicken stock. Season and let simmer over low heat for 6 minutes.

Mix together the milk and potato starch. Add the mixture to the pan as well as the Dijonnaise mustard. Let simmer for 5 minutes. Incorporate the pasta and parsley; mix well.

Serve in deep plates garnished with Parmesan cheese and anchovies.

PASTA SHELLS WITH SMOKED SALMON AND RED PEPPER SAUCE

4 SERVINGS

Preparation Time: 20 minutes

Cooking Time: none

1 tsp	(5 ml) Dijon mustard
2 tbsp	(25 ml) olive oil
1 tsp	(5 ml) red or white wine vinegar
	salt and pepper, to taste
6 oz	(18 g) smoked salmon, thinly sliced
1	green onion
1/4 cup	(50 ml) sliced celery
1 tbsp	(15 ml) capers (optional)
1	lemon, cut and peeled
1 tbsp	(15 ml) pesto
16	large shell pasta, cooked and hot

In a bowl, mix together the mustard, olive oil, and vinegar; season. Add the smoked salmon, green onion, celery, capers, lemon and pesto; mix well. Stuff the 16 pasta shells with this mixture and serve.

MICHELANGELO FARANDOLIS

10 SERVINGS

Preparation Time: 20 minutes

Cooking Time: 1 hour

1 tbsp	(15 ml) olive oil
2 tbsp	(25 ml) chopped shallots
1 tsp	(5 ml) minced garlic
1 cup	(250 ml) dry white wine or chicken stock, skimmed of fat
1 cup	(250 ml) chicken stock or fish stock, skimmed of fat
12 oz	(341 ml) clams, drained (reserve the liquid)
19 oz	(540 ml) tomatoes with fine herbs, peeled and crushed
2 tsp	(10 ml) cornstarch diluted in water
4 oz	(125 g) smoked salmon cut into thin strips
12	black olives, pitted
	salt and pepper, to taste
3 oz	(90 g) pennine pasta cooked and hot
3 oz	(90 g) ruote pasta, cooked and hot
3 oz	(90 g) ziti pasta, cooked and hot

GARNISH

1/2 cup	(125 ml) chopped artichoke hearts
1/2 cup	(125 ml) chopped hearts of palm
2 tbsp	(25 ml) chopped, fresh parsley

In a pan, heat the oil and sauté the shallots. Add the garlic, white wine, chicken stock and clam juice. Add the tomatoes and let simmer over low heat for 20 minutes. Thicken the sauce with cornstarch.

Incorporate the clams, smoked salmon and olives; season and keep warm.

Dress each plate with a mixture of the different pastas and cover with the sauce. Garnish with artichoke hearts, hearts of palm and parsley.

FARFALLE WITH A CREAMY SMOKED SALMON SAUCE

4 SERVINGS

Preparation Time: 15 minutes
Cooking Time: 15 minutes

2 tsp	(10 ml)	olive oil
2 tbsp	(25 ml)	chopped shallots
1		bay leaf
1		sprig of thyme
1		sprig of parsley
1 tsp	(5 ml)	black pepper
1 cup	(250 ml)	dry white wine
1 1/2 cups	(375 ml)	fish stock or chicken stock, skimmed of fat
1 tbsp	(15 ml)	melted butter
1 tbsp	(15 ml)	all-purpose flour
1/2 cup	(125 ml)	35% cream or 15% cream (if sauce is thick)
1 tbsp	(15 ml)	chopped chives
1 tbsp	(25 ml)	grated Parmesan cheese
6 oz	(180 g)	smoked salmon, cut into thin strips
1/2 lb	(250 g)	farfalle pasta, cooked and hot

GARNISH

1 cup	(250 ml)	sliced hearts of palm (optional)
1 cup	(250 ml)	chopped artichoke hearts (optional)
1		tomato, seeded and diced
6 to 8		chives

In a pan, heat the oil and sauté the shallots. Add the cluster of spices, garlic and pepper. Add the white wine and the fish or chicken stock. Let reduce by 1/3 and thicken with the mixture of butter and flour. Add the cream and let simmer for 1 to 2 minutes; strain.

Return the sauce to the pan. Add the chives, Parmesan cheese and smoked salmon; bring to a boil.

Garnish the farfalle pasta with the smoked salmon sauce, hearts of palm, artichoke hearts, diced tomatoes and chives.

VERMICELLI MEDLEY WITH FRESH MUSSELS

4 SERVINGS

Preparation Time: 20 minutes
Cooking Time: 10 minutes

24	mussels, cooked and shelled
4	sprigs of basil or parsley

MEDLEY

1 tbsp	(15 ml) olive oil
1	zucchini, julienned
1/2	green pepper, diced
1	green onion, sliced
1 tsp	(5 ml) minced garlic
1	tomato, seeded and diced
1/4 cup	(50 ml) grated Parmesan cheese
4 oz	(125 g) vermicelli, cooked and hot
1/4 cup	(50 ml) chopped, fresh basil or 1 tsp (5 ml) dry basil
1 tbsp	(15 ml) chopped, fresh oregano or 1/2 tsp (2 ml) dry oregano
1 tbsp	(15 ml) chopped, fresh parsley salt and pepper, to taste

VINAIGRETTE

1 tsp	(5 ml) Dijon mustard
1/3 cup	(75 ml) olive oil
1 tbsp	(15 ml) red or white wine vinegar
1 tbsp	(15 ml) lemon juice salt and pepper, to taste
1	tomato, seeded and diced
1/4 cup	(50 ml) chopped, fresh basil or 1 tsp (5 ml) dry basil
1 tsp	(5 ml) chopped, fresh oregano or 1 tsp (5 ml) dry oregano
1 tbsp	(15 ml) chopped, fresh parsley

MEDLEY

In a pan, heat the oil and sauté the zucchini, peppers and green onion. Add the garlic, diced tomatoes, cheese, vermicelli, basil, oregano and parsley; season. Set aside and let cool.

VINAIGRETTE

In a bowl, mix together the Dijon mustard, olive oil, vinegar and lemon juice; season. Add the diced tomatoes, basil, oregano and parsley.

Place the vermicelli in the middle of 4 plates. Surround with mussels and cover with vinaigrette. Garnish with fresh basil or parsley.

SPAGHETTI WITH MUSSELS AND MUSHROOMS

4 SERVINGS

Preparation Time: 15 minutes
Cooking Time: 12 minutes

1 tbsp	(15 ml) butter
2 tbsp	(15 ml) chopped shallots
2 cups	(500 ml) dry white wine
2 lb	(1 kg) mussels, scrubbed and debearded
2 tbsp	(25 ml) chopped, fresh parsley salt and pepper, to taste
1/2 lb	(250 g) spaghetti, cooked and hot
1	tomato, seeded and diced

SAUCE

2 tbsp	(25 ml) melted butter
2 tbsp	(25 ml) all-purpose flour
1/2 cup	(125 ml) 15% cream
1 lb	(250 g) cooked mushrooms
2 tbsp	(25 ml) chopped, fresh parsley

GARNISH

4	sprigs of parsley

In a large pot, melt the butter over high heat and lightly cook the shallots.

Add the mussels, white wine and parsley; season. Cover, reduce the heat, and let simmer for 3 to 5 minutes or until the mussels open. Shell the mussels and set aside. Reserve the cooking broth. Discard any unopened mussels.

SAUCE

In a pan, melt the butter and add the flour. Incorporate the cooking broth and let simmer for 5 minutes, while stirring.

Add the cream, mussels, mushrooms and parsley. Serve the spaghetti covered with sauce, and garnish with diced tomatoes and parsley.

SPAGHETTI WITH ZUCCHINI AND CRAB

4 SERVINGS

Preparation Time: 15 minutes
Cooking Time: 15 minutes

12 oz	(341 ml) beer
4	zucchini, washed
2 tbsp	(25 ml) olive oil
1/2 lb	(250 g) spaghetti, cooked and hot
2	green onions cut into round slices
1 tsp	(5 ml) minced garlic
1 1/2 cups	(375 ml) crab meat
1/2 cup	(125 ml) 15% cream
19 oz	(540 ml) tomatoes with fine herbs, crushed
1 tbsp	(15 ml) cornstarch salt and pepper, to taste freshly grated Sbrinz cheese, to taste

GARNISH

4	crab claws (optional)
4	sprigs of parsley

In a pan, reduce the beer by 75% and set aside.

On a cutting board, cut the zucchini into slices, lengthwise, and then cut into thin strips.

In a pan, heat the oil and sauté the zucchini and spaghetti. Add the onion and garlic. Add the crab meat, cream, beer and tomatoes. Bring to a boil. Thicken the sauce using cornstarch that has been diluted in a little water; season.

Place in a serving dish. Garnish with cheese, crab claws, and sprigs of parsley.

CARDINAL OF THE SEA LINGUINI

4 SERVINGS

Preparation Time: 15 minutes
Cooking Time: 8 minutes

2 cups	(500 ml) chicken stock, skimmed of fat
	salt and pepper, to taste
1/4 cup	(50 ml) sherry
2 tsp	(10 ml) lemon zest
2 tbsp	(25 ml) cornstarch
1 1/2 cups	(375 ml) milk
1/2 cup	(125 ml) grated Parmesan cheese
1 tbsp	(15 ml) fresh lemon juice
3 cups	(750 ml) lobster meat, cubed
1 lb	(500 g) linguini pasta, cooked and hot

In a saucepan, mix together the chicken stock, salt, pepper, sherry and lemon zest. Bring to a boil and let simmer over low heat for 3 to 5 minutes.

Dilute the cornstarch in milk and incorporate to the stock, stirring until thick. Remove from heat.

Add the Parmesan cheese, lemon juice, and lobster meat. Mix well and keep warm. Place the linguini on plates and cover with sauce. Serve immediately.

ITALIAN AROMA TAGLIATELLE

4 SERVINGS

Preparation Time: 20 minutes
Cooking Time: 25 minutes

1 tbsp	(15 ml) butter
2	garlic cloves, minced
8 oz	(226 ml) drained clams
19 oz	(540 ml) can of tomatoes with fine herbs
1/2 tsp	(2 ml) dried oregano
1 tsp	(5 ml) chopped, fresh coriander
1	medium egg, lightly beaten
2 cups	(250 ml) ricotta cheese
1/4 cup	(50 ml) grated Sbrinz cheese
1 tbsp	(15 ml) chopped, fresh parsley
	ground pepper, to taste
1 lb	(500 g) tagliatelle, cooked and hot

In a pan, melt the butter; add the garlic and clams and cook for 3 to 5 minutes. Add the tomatoes, the herbs and let simmer over low heat for 15 to 20 minutes, stirring occasionally.

In a bowl, mix together the egg, ricotta cheese, Sbrinz and parsley; season.

Place the tagliatelle on plates in the shape of a nest and place the cheese mixture in the middle. Cover with the sauce and serve hot.

MUSSELS AND FETTUCCINI WITH SUNDRIED TOMATOES

4 TO 6 SERVINGS

Preparation Time: 20 minutes

Cooking Time: 10 minutes

1/2 cup	(125 ml) sundried tomatoes (optional)
1/2 cup	(125 ml) corn oil
1 1/2 lb	(750 g) mussels, scrubbed and debearded
2 tbsp	(25 ml) butter
2 tbsp	(25 ml) chopped shallots
1 tsp	(5 ml) minced garlic
1 1/2 cups	(375 ml) dry white wine or water
	salt and pepper, to taste
1/2 lb	(250 g) fettuccini, cooked and hot
2	green onions cut into round slices
1	small red pepper, chopped
4	sprigs of fresh basil
2 tbsp	(25 ml) grated Parmesan cheese
1 tbsp	(15 ml) freshly ground black pepper
	hot sauce, to taste

SAUCE

2 tbsp	(25 ml) mustard
3 tbsp	(50 ml) corn oil
1 tbsp	(15 ml) red wine vinegar
3 tbsp	(50 ml) sour cream
1/2 cup	(125 ml) 15% cream
1 tbsp	(15 ml) minced garlic
	salt and pepper, to taste

In a small bowl, marinate the sundried tomatoes in oil for at least 20 minutes. Wash and clean the mussels; set aside.

In a large pan, melt the butter, and sauté the shallots. Add the garlic and white wine.

Add the mussels; season and cook over medium heat for 5 minutes or until the mussels open. Remove the mussels from the pan and let cool. Discard any mussels that do not open.

Keep 8 whole mussels for garnish and shell the others.

In a bowl, mix together all of the ingredients for the sauce and add the fettuccini, green onions, peppers and mussels. Toss well and season.

TIRAMISU

8 SERVINGS

Preparation Time: 25 minutes
Refrigeration Time: 24 hours

4	egg yolks
1/2 cup	(125 ml) sugar
1/4 cup	(50 ml) Kahlua liqueur
1 lb	(500 g) mascarpone cheese
4	egg whites
1/2 cup	(125 ml) sugar
1 1/2 cups	(375 ml) very strong, hot coffee
24	lady fingers or tea biscuits
2 tbsp	(25 ml) powdered cocoa, unsweetened

In a bowl, mix together the egg yolks and 1/2 cup (125 ml) of sugar. Whip until the eggs become fluffy. Add the Kahlua and cheese; set aside.

In another bowl, beat the egg whites to form soft peaks and fold into the egg yolk mixture. Once a smooth texture is obtained, set aside.

Dilute 1/2 cup (125 ml) of sugar in the coffee. Dip 12 ladyfingers or tea biscuits in the coffee, then place them side by side in the bottom of a 9 in (20 cm) Pyrex dish or in a medium sized ramekin. Spread half the cream mixture on the biscuits. Layer the other 12 biscuits, dipped in coffee, on top. Spread the remaining cream on top.

Sprinkle with cocoa and refrigerate for at least 24 hours.

ICED TORTONE WITH MACAROONS

8 TO 12 SERVINGS
Preparation Time: 15 minutes
Freezing Time: 8 hours

2 1/3 cups	(575 ml) crumbled Italian macaroons
1/4 cup	(50 ml) amaretto liqueur
2 cups	(500 ml) 15% cream
2 cups	(500 ml) vanilla cream
16	whole Italian macaroons

In a bowl, mix together 1 cup (250 ml) of crumbled macaroons, amaretto and cream. Whip the vanilla cream until it is firm and add to the mixture.

Pour the mixture into an aluminum loaf pan and freeze for at least 8 hours.

Remove from the pan by passing the outside of the mold under hot running water for a few seconds, and set on a platter. Let thaw for 2 minutes and cover the surface with the remaining crumbled macaroons. Place in the refrigerator until ready to serve.

Slice the Tortone and serve accompanied with Italian macaroons.

MOKA CAKE

8 TO 10 SERVINGS

Preparation Time: 40 minutes
Cooking Time: 25-30 minutes

1 cup	(250 ml) all-purpose flour
2 tsp	(10 ml) baking powder
1/2 tsp	(2 ml) salt
1/4 cup	(50 ml) finely chopped walnuts
2	egg whites
1/4 cup	(50 ml) sugar
2	egg yolks, beaten
1/2 cup	(125 ml) sugar
1/4 cup	(50 ml) hot water
1 tbsp	(15 ml) instant coffee granules
1 tbsp	(5 ml) vanilla extract

ICING

1/2 cup	(125 ml) softened butter
1/4 cup	(50 ml) very strong, cold coffee
2 1/4 cups	(550 ml) icing sugar
1 tsp	(5 ml) vanilla extract

Preheat the oven to 350°F (180°C). Grease and flour two round 8 in cake pans. In a bowl, mix together the flour, baking powder, salt and walnuts.

In another bowl, beat the egg whites until they form soft peaks, incorporating 1/4 cup (50 ml) of sugar.

In a small bowl, beat the egg yolks with 1/2 cup (125 ml) of sugar, and then add the coffee, dissolved in the hot water and vanilla.

Add the egg yolk mixture to the egg whites and fold in the flour. Be careful that the mixture does not fall.

Pour into the cake pans and bake for 25 to 30 minutes. Remove from the pans, and let cool. Cut each layer into three, horizontally.

Prepare the icing by mixing together the butter, coffee, icing sugar and vanilla. Spread a thin layer of icing on each layer of the cake, and then stack. Decorate with walnuts and whipped cream if desired.

TABLE OF CONTENTS